All you need to know about Laos

4

Introduction

Laos, officially the Lao People's Democratic Republic, is a landlocked country in Southeast Asia, bordered by Thailand to the west, Myanmar to the northwest, China to the north, Viet Nam to the east, and Cambodia to the south. With an area of about 236,800 square kilometers, Laos is the only landlocked country in Southeast Asia that does not directly border the sea. The capital of Laos is Vientiane, located on the banks of the Mekong River, which plays a central role in the country's geographical and cultural landscape.

The history of Laos dates back thousands of years, with early civilizations that existed more than 10,000 years ago in what is now Laos. Khmer rule shaped the region in the 1st millennium AD, followed by various Laotian kingdoms that flourished in the 14th to 18th centuries. Modern Laos was colonized by France in the 19th century and remained under French rule until independence in 1954.

The political structure of Laos is a one-party socialist republic in which the Lao Communist Party is the dominant political force. Since the 1975 revolution, Laos has developed a political system that is heavily influenced by communist ideologies and centralized control, while at the same time introducing economic reforms to modernize the country and fight poverty.

The population of Laos is made up of more than 7 million people, representing a variety of ethnicities and languages. According to the last census, the Lao are the largest ethnic group, followed by the Hmong, Khmu and other hill tribes. The cultural diversity is reflected in the traditions, customs, and religious practices that are heavily influenced by Theravada Buddhism, which is the dominant religion in the country.

The economy of Laos is mainly based on agriculture and natural resources such as wood and minerals. However, in recent years, the country has also seen progress in the tourism sector, with visitors mostly attracted by the country's natural beauty, historical sites, and people's hospitality.

Geographically, Laos is a country of contrasts, ranging from lush rainforests in the south to the mountainous landscapes in the north. The Mekong River, one of the largest rivers in the world, flows through the country and offers not only important trade routes, but also rich ecological diversity.

This book offers a comprehensive exploration of Laos, from its history and culture to its natural treasures and practical travel tips for visitors. It invites you to discover this unique country and understand how Laos is preserving its rich past while looking to a promising future.

Geography and climate of Laos

Laos, a landlocked country in Southeast Asia, covers an area of about 236,800 square kilometers and borders five neighboring countries: Thailand to the west and southwest, Myanmar to the northwest, China to the north, Viet Nam to the east, and Cambodia to the south. It is the only country in the region that does not directly border the sea. The geographical location of Laos between 14° and 23° north latitude and 100° and 108° east longitude strongly influences its climate and landscape.

The country can be roughly divided into three geographical regions: the plains on the banks of the Mekong River in the western part, the central mountain range that runs from northwest to southeast, and the eastern plateaus and mountains. One of the largest rivers in the world, the Mekong River runs through Laos for more than 1,800 kilometers and plays a central role in the lives of the people as well as in the country's economy. It serves as a transport route, energy source and water source for agriculture.

The central mountain range, also known as the Annamite Mountains, stretches for about 1,200 kilometers and forms the natural watershed between the Mekong Basin and the river systems that drain to the east. These mountains are mainly made of limestone and granite and reach heights of up to 2,800 meters, with Phou Bia being the highest peak in the country at 2,820 meters.

The eastern plateaus and mountains are characterized by a hilly landscape that extends to the border with Viet Nam. It is also home to the Bolaven Plateaus, known for their fertile soils and coffee plantations. The highest elevations in the east reach heights of about 1,800 meters above sea level.

The climate in Laos varies depending on the geographical location and altitude. In general, the climate can be divided into three main types: tropical monsoon climate, subtropical highland climate, and dry continental climate. Most areas in northern and central Laos experience a tropical monsoon climate with a distinct rainy and dry season. The rainy season lasts from May to October, while the dry season lasts from November to April. The southern regions, including the Bolaven Plateaus, have a subtropical climate with slightly more moderate temperatures and less pronounced rainy and dry seasons.

The natural environment of Laos is home to a rich variety of animal and plant species, including a variety of endemic species. The flora ranges from evergreen rainforests in the south to deciduous forests in the northern and central mountainous regions. The fauna includes elephants, bears, tigers, gibbons and numerous species of birds that live in the protected areas of the country.

Overall, the geography and climate of Laos is a fascinating interplay of geographical features that shape the way people live, support ecological diversity, and make Laos a unique destination in Southeast Asia.

History of Laos: From the Beginnings to Independence

The history of Laos spans a rich period of time that spans thousands of years and has shaped the country into a fascinating mosaic of cultural, political and social developments. Early human settlements in the region can be traced back to more than 10,000 years ago, with archaeological finds such as that of Ban Chiang offering important insights into the lives of the early inhabitants. Often referred to as the prehistoric and pre-colonial era, these early societies developed agricultural techniques and cultural traditions that remain the basis of Laotian society today.

In the 1st millennium AD, the Khmer Empire from what is now Cambodia exerted considerable influence on the region, including today's Laotian territories. The presence of Khmer rule is evidenced by monumental temples and archaeological remains in southern Laos, indicating significant cultural and political integration. This period marked a high point for Hinduism and Buddhism as major religions in the region.

From the 14th century onwards, independent kingdoms emerged in Laos, such as Lan

Xang, which was founded by King Fa Ngum. Lan Xang stretched over large parts of present-day Laos and parts of Thailand and Cambodia and experienced its heyday under King Setthathirat in the 16th century. During this time, important Buddhist temples and cultural centers such as Wat Phu and the city of Luang Prabang were built, which are still considered UNESCO World Heritage Sites today.

In the 18th century, the decline of Lan Xang began due to internal conflicts and external threats from the emerging Siamese kingdom. In the 19th century, Laos became a battlefield between the imperial powers France and Siam (now Thailand), who fought for influence and territory. In 1893, after the Franco-Siamese War, Laos was formally declared a protectorate of France and incorporated into the French Indochina colony.

During French colonial rule, Laos experienced profound social and economic changes that marked the beginning of modern administration and infrastructure, but also provoked local resentment and independence aspirations. After World War II, Laos became a central theater in the Indochina War, during which the struggle for independence and self-determination intensified.

On July 19, 1949, Laos officially gained sovereignty as an autonomous state within the French Union. However, the aspirations for complete independence were not realized until after the Indochina Wars and the negotiations in Geneva in 1954, which led to the neutralization and independence of Laos. This period laid the foundation for the modern political structure of the country, which still exists today as the Lao People's Democratic Republic and has developed economically, politically and socially over the decades.

Laos in the 20th Century: Colonial Rule and Independence Movements

Laos in the 20th century was marked by profound changes due to colonization, wars and the struggle for national independence. At the beginning of the century, Laos was part of the French colony of Indochina, which also included Viet Nam and Cambodia. The French considered Laos a valuable territory for economic exploitation, especially due to its natural resources such as timber and minerals, as well as its strategic location as a link between the other colonies and the motherland.

During colonial rule, the French introduced modernization measures, but these were often at the expense of the local population. The expansion of infrastructure and the introduction of new administrative systems had a positive impact on economic development on the one hand, but on the other hand they led to social inequalities and dissatisfaction among the population. This discontent intensified over time and paved the way for the first signs of an independence movement.

During World War II, Japanese troops occupied Laos after subjugating the French colonial administration. This period of occupation contributed to the radicalization of some Laotian nationalists who campaigned for an independent future from foreign rule. After the end of World War II and the defeat of Japan, Laos was once again placed under French control, further exacerbating tensions between the nationalist movements and the colonial administration.

The 1950s were marked by political instability as the Cold War increasingly affected Southeast Asia. Laos became the scene of a proxy conflict between the United States and the Soviet Union, with the Lao Communist Party, the Pathet Lao, receiving support from communist North Vietnam. At the same time, the United States supported the Laotian royal government, leading to a decades-long civil war that intensified in the 1960s and 1970s.

The Vietnam War had a devastating impact on Laos, which became the target of extensive bombing by the United States, which saw Laos as part of its efforts against communism. These bombings, which became known as the secret warfare chapter, left deep wounds in Laotian society and caused severe environmental damage. The war finally ended in 1975 with the victory of the communist forces leading the Pathet Lao.

On December 2, 1975, the Lao People's Democratic Republic was proclaimed, and the country entered an era of communist regime that is still in power today. The post-war period was marked by social and economic challenges, while Laos tried to modernize its economy and position itself in a globalized world. Despite these challenges, Laos has become a stable and peaceful country that strives to preserve its identity while striving for sustainable development.

Laos since independence: politics and society

Laos since independence in 1954 has undergone a complex political and social development, shaped by its role as a socialist one-party republic. After the end of colonial rule and the Indochina Wars, Lao's communist party, the Lao People's Revolutionary Party (LPRP), took over the political leadership of the country. The LPRP was founded by Pathet Lao fighters who had fought against the royal Laotian government and US intervention during the civil war.

The 1975 Constitution established Laos as a People's Democratic Republic and laid down the basic principles of the socialist system that still exists today. Politically, Laos is dominated by the LPRP, which functions as the country's only legal political party and plays a central role in government policy and decision-making. The president is elected every five years by the National Assembly, which in turn is controlled by the LPRP.

Over the past few decades, Laos has made significant progress in economic development and poverty reduction, with the country experiencing annual economic growth. The government has focused on improving infrastructure, especially in the field of road construction and energy supply, to promote economic integration and access to remote areas. Nevertheless, Laos remains one of the poorest countries in the region, with a sizeable population living below the poverty line, especially in rural areas.

The education system in Laos has also evolved, with literacy rates steadily increasing and access to primary and secondary education progressively improving. However, higher education remains inaccessible to many young people, and there is a need for further investment in educational institutions and teaching staff.

Socially, Laos is a multicultural country with several ethnic groups that maintain a diversity of traditions, languages and customs. The Lao form the largest ethnic group, followed by the Hmong, Khmu and other hill tribes, who often live in remote mountain regions. Despite this diversity, Theravada Buddhism is the dominant religion that shapes people's daily lives, customs, and moral values.

Laotian society is closely linked to nature and traditional agriculture, which continues to play an essential role in the livelihoods of many people. Traditional practices and cultural expressions, including music, dance and craftsmanship, are integral to the social fabric.

More recently, Laos has seen an increasing openness to foreign investment and tourism, with the tourism sector becoming an important economic factor. The government strives to find a balance between economic development and the protection of the natural environment, especially in the face of the threats posed by climate change and the exploitation of natural resources.

The political and social landscape of Laos remains dynamic and challenging as the country navigates its path into the future, striving to preserve its sovereignty, promote economic prosperity and achieve social justice.

Economy and development in Laos

The economy and development in Laos have undergone significant changes over the past decades, which have shaped the country on the way to a more modern and diversified economic structure. Laos is one of the least developed economies in Southeast Asia, heavily dependent on agriculture, which accounts for a significant portion of gross domestic product and employs much of the population. The main crops are rice, corn, coffee, cotton and sugar cane, which are mainly grown by smallholder farmers using traditional methods.

In recent years, the Laotian government has taken measures to increase agricultural productivity and reduce dependence on subsistence farming. This includes promoting modern farming methods, providing access to improved seed varieties and technologies, and developing irrigation systems. Despite these efforts, agriculture remains vulnerable to natural disasters such as droughts and floods, which can affect crop yields.

Another important industry in Laos is the extraction of natural resources, especially wood, minerals and hydropower. Laos has large areas of forest that offer rich timber resources, but are threatened due to illegal logging and uncontrolled exploitation. Mining also plays a role, with copper, gold, tin and bauxite being the main ore deposits, some of which are mined in cooperation with foreign companies.

A crucial area for Laos' economic development is the energy sector, especially hydropower. Due to its geographical location on the Mekong River and its numerous rivers, Laos has considerable potential for hydroelectric power plants that produce energy for both domestic demand and export. Large hydropower projects such as the Nam Theun 2 and the Xayaburi Dam are part of the country's efforts to expand its energy infrastructure and promote economic growth.

Tourism has also become an important economic sector, with Laos increasingly known as a destination for cultural and nature tourism. Visitors appreciate Luang Prabang's historical sites, the natural beauty of the Mekong River and surrounding landscapes, and the country's rich cultural diversity. The government has taken measures to promote the tourism sector, including improving infrastructure and promoting cultural heritage.

However, Laos' economic development faces challenges such as limited resources, dependence on foreign investment, and the need for improved education and health infrastructure. The government is working to diversify the economy and create a more favorable environment for investment in order to strengthen growth and improve the living conditions of the population. Overall, Laos' economy and development represent a dynamic mix of opportunities and challenges that the country must navigate on its path to sustainable and inclusive development.

The cultural diversity of Laos

The cultural diversity of Laos reflects the country's rich history, ethnic diversity, and deep-rooted traditions. As a multicultural state, Laos is home to a variety of ethnic groups, each with its own languages, customs, and cultural practices. The largest ethnic group is the Lao, who represent the dominant culture and language in the country. Laotian culture is strongly influenced by Theravada Buddhism, which plays a central role in people's daily lives and influences architecture, art, music and festivals.

In addition to the Lao, there are numerous ethnic minorities who live mainly in the mountainous regions of the country. These include the Hmong, Khmu, Akha, Yao, and many others, some of whom still retain traditional ways of life and rituals that have been passed down for generations. These ethnic groups contribute to cultural diversity and enrich the cultural heritage of Laos with their own dialects, crafts and folkloric traditions.

The traditional music and dance of Laos play an important role in the cultural identity of the country. Traditional musical instruments such as the khaen (a bamboo mouth organ), the angklung (an ensemble of bamboo tubes) and the saw (a type of lute) are typical of the Laotian musical tradition. Dance is also an important form of artistic expression, often associated with religious festivals or celebrations such as the Bun Pha Wet or the Bun Bang Fai, where dancers wear traditional costumes and perform ritual movements.

The architecture of Laos reflects the Buddhist influences as well as the historical connections to the Khmer and other regional cultures. Most of the traditional buildings, including temples and monasteries, are designed in the Lao style, which is characterized by curved roofs, decorative carvings, and ornate facades. Luang Prabang, a UNESCO World Heritage City, is famous for its well-preserved traditional buildings and is considered an outstanding example of Laotian architecture.

The cuisine of Laos is another facet of the country's cultural diversity, which is characterized by fresh ingredients, aromatic herbs and spices. Signature dishes such as the national dish laap (a type of minced meat salad), mok pa (steamed fish in banana leaves), sticky rice and various soups are popular and reflect the agrarian way of life and the availability of natural resources.

Religious holidays and festivals play a central role in the Laotian calendar, providing opportunities for fellowship, ancestor worship and traditional customs. The Pi Mai Lao New Year, celebrated in April, is a time of cheerfulness and purification, using water as a symbol of purification and renewal. Other significant festivals include religious ceremonies such as Visakha Bucha Day, which celebrates the birth, enlightenment, and death of the Buddha, as well as local festivals that celebrate regional customs and rituals.

Overall, the cultural diversity of Laos is a living testimony to the historical continuity, deep spiritual connection and artistic expression of a people who are proud of their traditions and strive to preserve them in an increasingly globalized world.

Religions in Laos: Buddhism and more

Religion plays a central role in Lao society, with Theravada Buddhism being the dominant religion. This Buddhist tradition, which originates mainly from Sri Lanka, has deep roots in Laotian culture and shapes the country's daily life, customs and social order. Buddhism was historically introduced through the influence of Buddhist missionaries from India and later from other Southeast Asian countries such as the Kingdom of Lanna in northern Thailand.

In Laos, there are a large number of temples and monasteries that serve as spiritual and cultural centers. These monasteries play an important role in the community, not only performing religious rituals and ceremonies, but also providing educational facilities for young monks and the local population. Monks play a respected role in society and are respected for their spiritual devotion and their teachings on morality and ethics.

In addition to Buddhism, Laos has a variety of folk religions and animistic beliefs, often associated with traditional rites and practices. These animist traditions reflect the belief in spirits, ancestral spirits, and nature spirits, which are considered part of the natural environment. Many Laotian families continue to practice these ancient customs by performing rituals to maintain the balance between man and nature.

Another significant religious minority in Laos are the Christians, who are mainly from the ethnic minorities and are active in different parts of the country. Christian communities have increased over time, especially in urban areas and among ethnic groups that have close ties with foreign missionaries.

Islam is another religious minority in Laos, although the Muslim population is relatively small compared to other religions. Most Muslim communities are concentrated in the south of the country, especially in Champasak province, where they have historical ties to Arab and Malay traders who traveled through the region during trade routes.

Religious festivals and celebrations play a significant role in the Laotian calendar, with special emphasis on Buddhist holidays such as Pi Mai (New Year), Visakha Bucha Day, and the Kathin ceremony. These festivals provide an opportunity for community, spiritual reflection and the strengthening of social bonds within the community.

Overall, the diversity of religions in Laos reflects the cultural richness and historical continuity of the country, while Laotian society preserves its traditions while navigating a globalized world.

Traditional Arts and Crafts in Laos

The traditional arts and crafts of Laos reflect the rich cultural heritage and craftsmanship of the people who have lived in this Southeast Asian country for centuries. Artisan traditions are deeply rooted in the daily life and identity of Laotian society, with each artwork and craft often telling a story that has lasted for generations.

A prominent feature of Laotian art is the elaborate textiles produced by the country's various ethnic groups. Women from the mountainous regions, such as the Hmong, Yao and Akha, are known for their skill in weaving and embroidery, often using complex patterns and traditional motifs. These textiles not only serve as clothing, but also have cultural significance and are often worn on festive occasions such as weddings and religious ceremonies.

Wood carving is another significant art form in Laos, often used in the production of temple decorations, religious figures, and traditional furniture. Artisans often use local woods such as teak and mahogany to create elaborate carvings decorated with religious symbols, mythological figures, and geometric patterns. These works of art add to the beauty and spiritual atmosphere of the temples and monasteries scattered throughout the country.

Ceramics and pottery also have a long tradition in Laos, with potters using clay to make vessels, tableware and decorative objects. Pottery is often practiced in rural communities, where clay is abundant and the techniques are passed down from generation to generation. Prized for their robustness and simple yet elegant designs, the pottery is made for both local use and trade.

Metalworking and blacksmithing are also traditional crafts in Laos, often used to make weapons, tools, and ritual items. The processing of silver and brass is particularly practiced by the ethnic minorities, who create elaborate jewelry and household items, often decorated with filigree patterns and engraved designs.

In addition to these traditional crafts, there is also a living tradition of painting and sculpture, which often depict religious themes and stories from Laotian mythology. Temple walls and ceilings are often adorned with colorful frescoes and murals that illustrate the life of the Buddha, celestial scenes, and symbolic representations of virtues and vices.

The traditional art forms and crafts of Laos are not only an expression of creativity and craftsmanship, but also an important part of the country's cultural identity and heritage. They add to the beauty of Laotian culture and continue to be nurtured and cherished as the country finds its place in the modern world.

The ethnic diversity of Laos

The ethnic diversity of Laos is a fascinating feature of the country, which includes a variety of ethnic groups, each with their own languages, traditions, and ways of life. The largest ethnic group is the Lao, who make up about two-thirds of the total population and live mainly in the central plains of the country. The Lao are closely connected to the Tai ethnic groups and speak the Laotian language, the official language of the country.

In addition to the Laos, there are more than 40 recognized ethnic minorities in Laos, who often live in the mountainous regions in the north and south of the country. These minorities include the Hmong, Khmu, Akha, Yao, and Lahu, among others, each with its own cultural identity and history. Many of these ethnic groups have retained their own dialects, traditions, religious beliefs, and craft traditions that have often been handed down for centuries.

The Hmong are one of the largest ethnic minorities in Laos and are known for their traditional textiles and embroidery, which use rich patterns and symbols that often have spiritual meanings. The Khmu are an indigenous group that traditionally lives in the mountains and forests and feeds mainly on subsistence agriculture and hunting. The Akha are known for their skillful agriculture and cultural practices, while the Yao are often known for their knowledge of medicine and manual skills.

The ethnic diversity of Laos contributes to the cultural richness of the country and is reflected in a variety of religious practices, traditional festivals and culinary traditions. Despite the cultural diversity, Laos has a common identity as a nation, which is fostered by the government's efforts to preserve ethnic harmony and cultural heritage.

However, the challenges of modernization and economic development have an impact on the traditional ways of life and the social structure of ethnic communities in Laos. The government strives for a balanced integration of ethnic minorities into the national development process, while respecting their cultural identity and their rights to self-determination.

Overall, the ethnic diversity of Laos is an important aspect of national identity and a legacy of the diversity and strength of the diverse communities that inhabit the country. As Laos moves forward into a globalized future, the recognition and promotion of ethnic diversity remains an essential part of national politics and society.

The Laotian language and its peculiarities

The Lao language, also known as Lao or Lao, is the official and dominant language in Laos. It belongs to the Tai Kadai language family and is closely related to the Thai and Isan dialects in Thailand. The Laotian alphabet is based on the Indian Brahmi script and was historically introduced by Buddhist missionaries from India.

A characteristic feature of the Laotian language is its tonal language, which means that the meaning of a word varies by the tone with which it is pronounced. There are six tones in Laotian: high, medium, low, falling, rising and descending tone, each of which can change the meaning of a word. This often makes pronunciation challenging for non-native speakers, but for Lao speakers, pitch is an intuitive part of their communication.

The Laotian language has a rich vocabulary that is characterized by its close connection with Buddhist culture and historical interaction with other regional languages. Many religious terms, ritual expressions, and cultural concepts are an integral part of the Laotian vocabulary, often using metaphorical and figurative language.

Grammatically, Lao is an isolating language, which means that words usually do not undergo alterations through affixes or endings to indicate their grammatical function. Instead, Laotian uses word order and particles to convey meaning and express grammatical relationships between words.

The Laotian writing system is usually written with an alphabet consisting of 27 consonants and 8 vowels, each of which can be used in combinations to represent the sounds of the language. Although Laotian is historically documented through Buddhist texts and religious scriptures, modern Laotian literature has developed in various genres such as poetry, prose, and theater, often exploring cultural and social issues.

The Laotian language plays a crucial role in Laos' national identity and is actively promoted by educational institutions and media. Despite increasing globalization and the use of English as a second language, Lao remains a central part of daily life, culture, and communication in Laos, and is promoted by the government as a symbol of national unity and cultural continuity.

Food and Drink in Laos: A Culinary Journey

Food and drink in Laos offer a fascinating culinary journey through the rich variety of flavors that characterize the local cuisine. Laotian cuisine is heavily influenced by the country's natural resources, which offer an abundance of fresh ingredients such as rice, herbs, vegetables, river fish, and wild venison. One of the key ingredients in the Laotian diet is sticky rice, which is often served as an accompaniment to almost any dish and is considered a symbol of prosperity and abundance.

A characteristic feature of Laotian dishes is their simplicity and focus on fresh flavors and spices. Laap, a traditional minced meat salad, is one of Laos' national dishes and is made with minced meat (often chicken, beef, or fish) seasoned with lime juice, fish sauce, chili, and roasted rice powder. This blend of hot, sour, and spicy flavors is typical of Laotian cuisine and reflects a preference for balanced flavor profiles.

Another popular specialty in Laos is mok pa, a steamed fish cooked in banana leaves with herbs, chili, and coconut milk. This dish is an example of the creative use of natural

37

ingredients and traditional preparation methods that enrich the country's food culture. Soups also play an important role in the Laotian diet, including the spicy tom yam soup and the traditional pho soup, which is often enjoyed for breakfast.

Laotian cuisine also shows influences from neighboring countries, especially Thailand and Viet Nam, which contribute to the variety of dishes available. This culinary diversity is often accentuated by the use of fresh herbs such as coriander, mint and Thai basil, which add an aromatic touch to dishes and enhance the taste.

In rural areas, the diet often remains simple and seasonal, with people using traditional methods of food preservation such as drying meat and fish to supplement the diet during the rainy season. Wild vegetables and edible plants collected in the forests also play an important role in the diet of many rural communities.

As for drinks, Laotian coffee, often known as the "coffee of the Four Thousand Islands", is a local specialty prized for its bold flavor and rich texture. Lao-Lao, a traditional rice liquor, is also widely used and is often enjoyed on special occasions and festivals, with each region having its own variations and flavors.

Overall, eating and drinking in Laos offers not only a delicious culinary experience, but also a glimpse into the country's cultural diversity and agricultural tradition. The appreciation for fresh ingredients, the careful preparation of dishes and the importance of meals as a social ritual contribute to the rich gastronomic landscape of Laos, which visitors and locals alike can enjoy.

Nature and biodiversity in Laos

The nature and biodiversity in Laos are characterized by extraordinary diversity and reflect the rich ecological landscape of the country. Located in the heart of Southeast Asia, Laos is home to an impressive variety of ecosystems, ranging from tropical rainforests to mountain ranges and river landscapes. These natural habitats provide a home for a wide variety of animal and plant species, many of which are unique and endemic to the region.

The tropical rainforests of Laos are particularly remarkable and represent one of the last intact forest landscapes in the world. They are home to a variety of animal species, including elephants, tigers, leopards, bears, and a variety of monkey species. Many of these animals are endangered or threatened with extinction due to poaching, habitat loss and illegal timber harvesting. However, the government of Laos has taken measures to protect biodiversity, including the establishment of national parks and nature reserves.

The rivers and waterways in Laos play a crucial role in the country's ecosystem and support rich aquatic biodiversity. One of the longest rivers in the world, the Mekong River crosses Laos and provides habitat for a variety of fish species, including the rare and endangered Mekong giant catfish. The rivers also serve as important transport routes and contribute to the country's agricultural production, while at the same time providing a significant source of fisheries and livelihoods for the rural population.

The mountainous regions of Laos are also of great ecological importance and provide habitat for a variety of plants and animals adapted to the high altitudes and cooler climate. These mountain ranges are often covered by dense forests and help regulate the water cycle that supports the country's agricultural production and drinking water supply.

Biodiversity in Laos also includes a variety of plant species, including many medically and ecologically important species. The traditional medicine of Laotian culture uses many of these plants for their healing properties, which have often been passed down from generation to generation for centuries. Agricultural practice in Laos also includes the cultivation of rice, vegetables, and fruits in the country's fertile valleys and plains, with traditional methods of irrigation and land use being widespread.

Overall, nature and biodiversity in Laos is a valuable heritage that must be protected and preserved to serve future generations. The challenges of climate change, population growth and economic development require a sustainable use of natural resources and a responsible environmental management policy to preserve the unique diversity of Laos' flora and fauna.

The flora of Laos: flora and nature conservation

The flora of Laos is characterized by a variety of plant species that are adapted to the different climatic conditions and geographical regions of the country. Laos, as part of the Indo-Malaysian Biodiversity Hotspot, is home to a remarkable diversity of tropical rainforests, dry forests, savannahs, wetlands, and mountainous landscapes, each supporting its own unique flora and fauna regions.

The tropical rainforests of Laos are dominated by evergreen tree species such as teak, mahogany, tropical wood species and Dipterocarpaceae, which are important sources of wood and other forest products. These forests are also rich in epiphytic plants such as orchids, ferns and mosses, adapted to the high humidity and shady conditions of the forest crowns.

The dry forests and savannahs in the southern and central plains of Laos are characterized by tree-covered grass savannahs, which are characterized by fires during the dry season. These ecosystems support a variety of plant species such as acacias, palm trees, grasses, and herbaceous plants that are adapted to the seasonal dry periods.

Laos' river and freshwater systems are home to a variety of aquatic plant species, including water lilies, reeds, and water lilies, which provide important habitats and food sources for fish and other aquatic life. The country's natural wetlands play a crucial role in water retention, filtering pollutants, and supporting biodiversity.

The mountainous regions of Laos, especially in the north, are covered by montane forests characterized by a variety of evergreen and deciduous tree species. These forests are often rich in bamboo species, rhododendrons, and other alpine plants adapted to the altitude and cool climate. The montane forests contribute to the regulation of the water balance by storing water and releasing it during the rainy season, which is crucial for agricultural irrigation and protection against soil erosion.

Conservation of Laoss Flora is a priority of the government, which has created various nature reserves and national parks to conserve biodiversity and ecosystem services. These protected areas also serve as research centers for scientists and botanists to study and document plant diversity, as well as tourist attractions that offer visitors the opportunity to experience the natural beauty and ecological richness of Laos.

The challenges for protecting the flora of Laos include illegal logging, the conversion of forests to agricultural land, and the effects of climate change that threaten natural habitats. The sustainable use of natural resources and the protection of biodiversity therefore remain central issues for the future of Laos and its unique flora.

The fauna of Laos: wildlife and protected areas

The fauna of Laos is rich in diversity and includes an impressive range of animal species adapted to the country's different ecosystems. Due to its diverse landscapes and tropical climate, Laos provides habitats for a variety of mammals, birds, reptiles, amphibians, and fish, many of which are endemic or rare.

The tropical rainforests of Laos are home to some of the country's most remarkable animal species. Among them are the Asian elephant, the tiger, the leopard, the sun bear and various species of monkeys such as gibbons and macaques. These forests are also home to a variety of bird species, including the collared parakeet, hornbill and green woodpecker, known for their colourful plumage and diverse songs.

Laos' rivers and waterways support rich aquatic fauna, including the rare Mekong giant catfish, one of the largest freshwater fish species in the world. In addition to fish, the rivers also provide habitat for crocodiles, turtles and a variety of waterfowl that populate the banks and currents.

The mountainous regions of Laos, especially in the north, are home to a variety of animal species adapted to the cooler altitudes and alpine conditions. These include the serow, a type of goat, as well as various species of deer, bears and wild boars. These mountain ecosystems are also habitats for rare bird species such as the kalao and the imperial eagle, which are often found in inaccessible mountain forests.

The protection of Laos' fauna is of great importance for the preservation of the country's biodiversity. The government of Laos has established various protected areas and national parks to protect endangered species and preserve their natural habitats. These include Nam Et-Phou Louey National Park, Bolaven Plateau National Park and Nam Ha National Park, each of which is home to unique animal and plant species and serves as refuges for endangered species.

Despite these protective measures, Laos' fauna faces various threats, including poaching, habitat loss due to deforestation and agricultural conversion, and the effects of climate change. The illegal trade in wildlife and its products remains a challenge for wildlife conservation in Laos, and the government is working closely with international organizations to combat these practices and strengthen the protection of the country's fauna.

The sustainable use of natural resources and the protection of wildlife remain crucial for the future of Laos and its unique and diverse fauna. By promoting environmental awareness and supporting conservation efforts, Laos' rich ecosystems and wildlife diversity can be preserved for generations to come.

National parks and nature reserves in Laos

National parks and nature reserves in Laos play a crucial role in protecting the country's rich biodiversity and natural resources. Laos has a variety of protected areas that serve to conserve endangered species, support ecological processes, and maintain environmental integrity. These areas encompass a variety of ecosystems, including tropical rainforests, dry forests, wetlands, mountainous landscapes, and river ecosystems, each with their own unique challenges and conservation goals.

One of the most famous national parks in Laos is the Nam Et-Phou Louey National Park in the north of the country. This park is known for its variety of wildlife, including tigers, Asian elephants, gibbons, and numerous species of birds. The park serves as a refuge for endangered species and promotes sustainable ecotourism as a source of income for local communities involved in protecting nature.

The Phou Khao Khouay National Park, near the capital Vientiane, is another important protected area in Laos. It protects a variety of habitats, including forests, rivers and waterfalls, which perform important ecological functions and provide habitat for endangered species such as the Indochinese leopard. The park is also known for its biodiversity of plants and birds, offering visitors the chance to experience the natural beauty of Laos.

The Bolaven Plateau is a region in southern Laos that is known for its coffee plantations and waterfalls and also plays an important role in nature conservation. The Bolaven Plateau National Park protects the region's unique flora and fauna, including rare bird species such as the yellow-crowned parrot and the Siamese fireback.

Other nature reserves in Laos include Nam Ha National Park near Luang Namtha, which is known for its biodiversity of plants, birds and mammals, and Dong Hua Sao National Park near Pakse, which protects rare primate species such as the silver langur.

The Government of Laos works closely with international organizations and non-governmental organizations to strengthen the protection and management of these protected areas. This includes promoting sustainable development practices, raising environmental awareness among the population and combating illegal activities such as poaching and illegal logging.

The challenges facing nature reserves in Laos include pressure from population growth, the effects of climate change, and the need for sustainable use of natural resources to support local communities. By protecting and responsibly managing these areas, Laos can preserve its rich biodiversity while ensuring ecological services for society.

The Mekong region: lifeline and trade route

The Mekong region plays a central role in the geography, culture and economy of Laos and is considered a lifeline and trade route for the country and the surrounding regions of Southeast Asia. One of the longest rivers in the world, the Mekong River stretches for 4,350 kilometers and flows through six countries: China, Myanmar, Laos, Thailand, Cambodia and Viet Nam. In Laos, the Mekong River stretches for about 1,835 kilometers and forms the natural border with Thailand in the west.

The river plays a crucial role in the lives of people along its banks, providing water for irrigation of fields and fishing, and serving as a transport route for trade. For rural communities in Laos in particular, the Mekong is a vital resource that supports agriculture and secures livelihoods for many people.

The Mekong region is known for its diverse ecology and is home to a rich biodiversity of fish, birds, reptiles and plants. The river and its tributaries provide habitat for rare species such as the Mekong giant catfish, which is one of the largest freshwater fish in the world, as well as migratory birds that rest during their annual migrations.

Historically, the Mekong River has served as a major trade route that facilitated the exchange of goods, ideas, and cultures between the countries of Southeast Asia. The river landscapes and surrounding plains were shaped by the trade of products such as rice, silk, spices, timber and precious stones, with trading cities along the Mekong such as Luang Prabang and Vientiane becoming centres of trade and cultural flourishing.

Today, the Mekong River plays an important role in regional trade and economic integration. The countries along the river have established joint initiatives such as the Mekong River Commission (MRC) to promote sustainable use of water resources, monitor environmental impacts and strengthen cooperation in river basin governance.

Despite its importance, the Mekong River faces challenges from climate change, water pollution and pressure from the expansion of hydropower projects. These developments can have both environmental and socio-economic impacts on the region and require careful and balanced planning for the future of the river and its communities.

The Mekong region therefore remains not only a lifeline for the people and nature of Laos, but also a symbol of the connectedness and common challenges of the countries of Southeast Asia as they strive to ensure the sustainable development and protection of this unique river system.

The capital Vientiane: history and modernity

Vientiane, the capital of Laos, combines a rich history with modern developments that shape the cultural and economic center of the country. Located on the banks of the Mekong River, the city has a long history dating back to the 14th century, when it was established as a trading post and later the capital of the Lan Xang Kingdom. Under the reign of King Setthathirath in the 16th century, Vientiane flourished as a cultural and religious center, which is reflected in the magnificent temples and palaces that remain to this day.

The colonial era brought significant changes to Vientiane as Laos came under French rule. The city became an administrative center and underwent an architectural transformation with European influences, which is still visible today in the colonial buildings and boulevard-like streets. After independence in 1954, Vientiane began a period of growth and modernization, with the creation of new neighborhoods, transportation infrastructure, and educational institutions to meet the needs of a growing population.

Today, Vientiane is a melting pot of tradition and modernity, where historic sites such as

Wat Phra Kaew, which originally housed the Emerald Buddha, coexist with modern buildings, shops, and restaurants. The city has become an important economic and administrative center that attracts companies, diplomats and international organizations. The construction of the Friendship Bridge across the Mekong River has strengthened trade links with Thailand and made Vientiane an important hub in the regional economy.

Culturally, Vientiane is influenced by Buddhism, which plays a central role in the daily life of the people. Numerous temples and pagodas, such as Pha That Luang, a national symbol and one of the most important Buddhist sanctuaries in Laos, testify to the spiritual importance of the city. Traditional festivals and ceremonies, such as the Bun Pha Wet Festival, which marks the beginning of Buddhist Lent, are important cultural events that strengthen the social fabric of the city.

However, Vientiane's urban development faces challenges such as traffic congestion, pollution, and urban planning that require sustainable development. The government of Laos is committed to promoting environmental protection measures and improving the quality of life in the capital, while preserving the city's historical and cultural heritage.

Overall, Vientiane reflects the dynamic development and diversity of Laos, where history and modernity meet to create a vibrant metropolis that fascinates and attracts both locals and visitors alike.

Luang Prabang: Capital of Culture and UNESCO World Heritage Site

Luang Prabang, the former royal capital of Laos, is a gem of cultural and historical significance that impresses both locals and visitors with its beauty and heritage. The city is picturesquely located at the confluence of the Mekong and Nam Khan rivers and has been declared a World Heritage Site by UNESCO due to its rich cultural heritage. Its history dates back to the 7th century, when it was founded as the center of the Lane Xang Kingdom.

Luang Prabang experienced its heyday during the reign of the Lan Xang kings in the 14th to 16th centuries and became an important religious center of Theravada Buddhism. Numerous temples and monasteries have been built, including Wat Xieng Thong, which is considered one of the most important examples of Laotian temple architecture. These magnificent structures are well preserved to this day and attract pilgrims and tourists alike.

The colonial era brought further architectural influences to Luang Prabang, especially by the French, who erected numerous colonial buildings in the French colonial style, which still characterize the urban landscape. The historic character of the city is evident in the narrow streets, traditional wooden houses and the colorful markets that enliven urban life.

Religious celebrations and festivals are an integral part of life in Luang Prabang. Particularly important is the Tak Bat, the monks' morning alms collection, where believers offer food and donations as a sign of veneration and care. The annual Boun Ok Phansa Festival, which marks the end of Buddhist Lent, attracts thousands of worshippers and visitors who want to witness the colorful processions and ceremonies.

In addition to its cultural significance, Luang Prabang is also known for its natural beauty, which is characterized by lush green hills and waterfalls that can be found around the city. Kuang Si Waterfall, located about 29 kilometers southwest of Luang Prabang, is a popular destination for visitors who want to enjoy the picturesque pools and turquoise waters of the waterfall.

The city has become a major tourist destination in recent decades, resulting in an increasing number of hotels, restaurants, and shops aimed at meeting the needs of visitors while preserving Luang Prabang's unique culture and traditions. The government of Laos and local organizations are working together to promote sustainable tourism while protecting the city's historical and natural treasures to ensure that Luang Prabang remains a source of inspiration and admiration for generations to come.

Savannakhet: Historical Heritage and Colonial Architecture

Savannakhet, the second largest city in Laos, is a fascinating mix of historical heritage and colonial architecture that tells its own unique story. The city is located in the southern part of Laos and borders Thailand, which made it an important trading point along the historic Silk Road. Founded in the 17th century, Savannakhet flourished during the reign of the Lan Xang Kingdom and served as an important trading city along the Mekong River.

During the colonial period, Savannakhet became a center of French administration and trade. This is clearly reflected in the city's architecture, with colonial mansions, French colonial-style buildings, and wide boulevards dominating the cityscape. Its historical significance as a trading center can still be felt today in the well-preserved buildings and streets of Savannakhet, which offer a glimpse into Laos' colonial past.

In addition to colonial architecture, Savannakhet is also known for its cultural treasures, including Buddhist temples such as the That Ing Hang Stupa, which is a significant religious site for believers from the region. The stupa is known for its architectural beauty and spiritual significance, which is a source of contemplation and prayer for the local population and visitors.

The city is also a center for education and culture in Laos, with several schools and universities promoting educational and cultural programs. Savannakhet is home to a variety of artisans who cultivate traditional crafts such as weaving, ceramics and silversmithing that have been passed down for generations.

Savannakhet is part of a larger regional initiative to promote tourism and economic development, with local and international investments aimed at improving infrastructure and creating new opportunities for visitors. The city has established itself as an attractive destination for culturally interested travelers who want to experience the rich history, architecture, and hospitality of the Laotian community.

More recently, the government of Laos has taken measures to strengthen the protection and preservation of Savannakhet's historical heritage by supporting restoration projects and improving access to cultural resources. These efforts reflect a commitment to preserving Savannakhet's unique identity and history, while promoting the city's development as a modern center for culture and tourism.

Pakse and the surrounding area: Gateway to the south of Laos

Pakse, a major city in southern Laos, acts as a gateway to the picturesque surroundings and is an important hub for trade, culture, and tourism. Located at the confluence of the Mekong and Sedone Rivers, Pakse offers not only a strategic geographical location but also a rich cultural history dating back to the times of the Champasak Kingdom.

The city itself was founded in the late 19th century under French colonial rule and quickly developed into a trading center for the surrounding agricultural regions. Even today, Pakse is an important market for agricultural products such as coffee, tea, rubber and fruits produced by the surrounding provinces.

Pakse is also known for its traditional architecture, which is a mix of French colonial buildings and Laotian architecture. The city is home to several significant Buddhist temples and stupas, including Wat Luang and Wat Phabad, which are important religious centers for the local population.

The surroundings of Pakse are characterized by a breathtaking landscape of lush forests, rice fields and picturesque rivers. Just a few kilometers south of the city is the Bolaven

Plateau, known for its cool climate, waterfalls, and coffee plantations. Tad Fane Waterfall and Tad Yuang Waterfall are popular destinations for visitors who want to experience the natural beauty of the region. Another highlight of the area around Pakse is the 4,000 islands in the Mekong, a group of islands and sandbanks that stretch over an extensive stretch of the river. These islands, including Don Det and Don Khon, are known for their laid-back atmosphere, opportunities for swimming and kayaking, and the opportunity to spot the rare Irrawaddy dolphins that live in the shallow waters of the Mekong River.

In terms of tourism, Pakse has gained in importance in recent years, with investments in infrastructure and accommodation increasing the attractiveness of the region as a tourist destination. New hotels, restaurants and tour operators have established themselves to cater to the growing influx of visitors who want to discover the diversity of the cultural, historical and natural treasures of Pakse and its surroundings.

The government of Laos is actively committed to the sustainable development of the region by implementing programs to promote tourism and protect natural resources. These efforts are critical to preserving Pakse's unique heritage while maximizing economic benefits for the local population.

Journey through the provinces of Laos: From north to south

Laos, a country with a rich cultural diversity and breathtaking scenic beauty, stretches from the mountains in the north to the fertile plains in the south along the Mekong River. A journey through the provinces of Laos offers a fascinating insight into the different regions and ways of life of the Laotian population.

In the north of the country lies the province of Phongsaly, known for its mountainous landscape and the ethnic diversity of its population. It is home to numerous ethnic minorities, including the Hmong, Akha and Tai Lü, who preserve their own traditions, languages and ways of life. The capital Phongsaly offers a glimpse into the daily life of the mountain people and is a starting point for trekking tours to remote villages and traditional markets.

Further south is Luang Namtha Province, known for its lush forests and Nam Ha National Park, which is home to a variety of ecosystems and is a paradise for nature lovers and adventurers. The city of Luang Namtha is a center for ecotourism and offers opportunities for hiking, kayaking and meeting the local people.

The province of Oudomxay, also located in the north, is characterized by its terraced rice fields and traditional villages that preserve the culture of the Khmu and Hmong ethnic groups. It is also home to Nam Kat Yola Pa National Park, known for its waterfalls and unique wildlife, including gibbons and elephants.

Centrally located in Laos is Xieng Khouang Province, famous for the Plain of Jars, an archaeological site that includes hundreds of prehistoric stone sarcophagi whose purpose and origin are still a mystery. The capital, Phonsavan, offers access to these mysterious artifacts, as well as historical sites from recent history that commemorate the effects of the Vietnam War.

The capital Vientiane, located in the center of the country on the Mekong River, is a cultural and administrative center that offers a mix of colonial architecture, Buddhist temples and modern developments. Here you will find important sights such as Wat Phra Keo and That Luang Stupa, which have historical and religious significance.

The southern province of Savannakhet, near the border with Thailand, is known for its colonial architecture and the historical heritage of the Champasak Kingdom. The city of Pakse, also located in the south, serves as a gateway to the picturesque surroundings of the Bolaven Plateau and the 4,000 islands in the Mekong, which are prized for their natural beauty and cultural significance.

This journey through the provinces of Laos shows the diversity and beauty of this country, which impresses with its landscapes, history and cultural heritage. Each region has its own stories to tell, offering visitors an unforgettable experience that captures the essence of Laos and reflects the hospitality of its people.

Festivals and celebrations in Laos

Festivals and celebrations in Laos are a vibrant expression of the country's rich cultural traditions and spiritual practices, which are deeply rooted in Buddhist philosophy. One of the most important festivals is the Pi Mai Lao, the Laotian New Year, which is celebrated in April and lasts for three days. During this time, families come together to clean homes, visit Buddha statues, and pour water over Buddha's images to ask for blessings and good luck for the coming year.

Another important festival is the Boun Bang Fai, the Festival of Rockets, which is celebrated in the northern provinces to celebrate the beginning of the rainy season. The locals build large rockets out of bamboo and let them rise into the sky, accompanied by music, dancing and traditional games. This feast is also a time of prayer for abundant rain and a successful harvest.

Luang Prabang hosts the Boun Ok Phansa Festival, which marks the end of Buddhist Lent. During this festival, monks and worshippers gather for solemn processions, where colorful lanterns are carried through the streets and the stupa of Wat Xieng Thong is illuminated. It is a time of prayer, offerings, and spiritual renewal.

The That Luang Festival in Vientiane is an annual event that celebrates the importance of the That Luang Stupa, one of the country's most sacred landmarks. Thousands of devotees flock together to pray, meditate, and make offerings, while the atmosphere is filled with Buddhist hymn music. The festival is also an opportunity for traditional dances, musical performances, and local handicraft exhibitions.

In addition to religious festivals, there are also cultural events that celebrate the ethnic diversity of Laos. The Hmong New Year Festival, celebrated by the Hmong community, is a colorful event with traditional dances, chants, and craft markets that express the rich culture and history of this ethnic group.

Every festival in Laos is an opportunity for community and cohesion, where traditions are nurtured and passed down through generations. People celebrate with great dedication and joy to preserve their cultural identity while welcoming guests from all over the world who want to experience the country's unique customs and celebrations.

Music and dance in Laotian culture

Music and dance play a central role in the cultural identity of Laos, a country rich in traditions and historical depth. The traditional music of Laos is strongly influenced by Buddhist and animist influences and reflects the diversity of ethnic groups that inhabit the country. Typical musical instruments include the khene, a kind of mouth organ made of bamboo, as well as drums, gongs and flutes.

Traditional Laotian music is often played at religious ceremonies, festivals and ritual occasions to promote spiritual harmony and well-being. These pieces of music are often passed down orally from generation to generation and are closely linked to the Laotian language and literature, which are often transmitted in the form of songs and poems.

Different styles of music and dance forms have developed in the different regions of Laos, reflecting local traditions and ways of life. For example, the dances of the Lao Lum people living in the central part of the country are characterized by gentle movements and elegant gestures, while the dances of the Hmong and other hill tribes have a more energetic and powerful form of expression.

Modern Laotian music has also evolved, integrating Western influences, especially from pop and rock music. Local bands and artists combine traditional instruments with modern sounds and lyrics in Lao and English to appeal to a wider audience and preserve cultural heritage.

Dance plays as important a role as music in Laotian culture, with traditional dances often performed at celebrations, festivals and cultural events. These dances are often accompanied by colorful costumes that reflect the cultural identity and history of each ethnicity.

Some of the most well-known traditional dances in Laos include the Lamvong, a circle dance in which couples twist and move to the rhythm of the music, and the Fon Tien, a ritual dance performed at ceremonies and religious festivals to appease spirits and bring good luck.

Overall, music and dance in Laos are more than just entertainment; they are a living expression of the country's cultural identity, history, and spiritual practices. They play an important role in connecting communities, preserving traditions and preserving Laos' unique cultural heritage for future generations.

Textile Art in Laos: Weaving and Traditional Patterns

Textile art in Laos has a long and significant history that is closely linked to the traditional ways of life and cultural values of the country's various ethnic groups. The craft of weaving and the creation of traditional patterns are an integral part of Laotian culture, carrying both practical and symbolic significance.

Women play a central role in Laotian textile art, as weaving has traditionally been a task that has been passed down from generation to generation. In many Laotian communities, weaving is an essential part of the social fabric and a significant source of income for women, who often work in cooperative groups or at home.

The traditional weaving techniques in Laos mainly include hand weaving on simple wooden frame or floor looms. These techniques require skill and patience, as weaving is often time-consuming and requires precise manual labor to create complex patterns and designs.

A characteristic feature of Laotian textile art is the traditional patterns, which often have symbolic meanings and are closely linked to the culture and beliefs of the respective community. Each ethnic race has its own typical designs and color combinations that can tell stories about the origin, history, and social status of the wearers.

The most famous textiles in Laos are the hand-woven silk and cotton fabrics, which are prized for their fineness, durability and aesthetic beauty. Silk, especially the hand-spun and dyed silk, is one of the most precious and sought-after materials in Laotian textile art and is often used for formal occasions such as weddings and Buddhist ceremonies.

Some of the traditional patterns commonly found in Laotian textiles are the "Sinh" pattern, which is typical of traditional Laotian skirts, as well as the "Mat me" pattern, which is created by the complex tying technique to create geometric or figurative designs. These patterns are often dyed with natural dyes derived from plants, minerals and insects, which gives the textiles a special depth and vibrancy.

Textile art in Laos is not only a means of producing clothing and home textiles, but also an important carrier of cultural heritage and identity. The art of weaving and the use of traditional patterns are an integral part of Laos' cultural heritage, which continues to be protected and promoted through initiatives to promote craftsmanship and sustainable development.

Handicraft Traditions in Laos: Silversmithing and Wood Carving

The artisanal traditions in Laos are deeply rooted in the history and culture of the country, which is rich in artistic talent and traditional skills. Two outstanding craft traditions that are particularly cultivated in Laos are silversmithing and wood carving.

Silversmithing in Laos has a long history and is known for its fine craftsmanship and artistic design. The silversmiths use traditional techniques and tools to create intricate designs on silver sheet, often inspired by floral motifs, animal representations, or mythological figures. This art form not only has aesthetic significance, but also plays a ritual and symbolic role in religious ceremonies and traditional festivals.

Wood carving is another important craft tradition in Laos, which manifests itself in the design of religious sculptures, architectural elements and everyday objects. Laotian woodcarvers are known for their ability to create ornate ornaments and detailing from wood, often decorated with intricate geometric patterns and mythological motifs. These works of art not only serve as decoration, but are also an expression of the country's spiritual and cultural identity.

The materials used for these crafts are often locally sourced and hand-picked. Silversmiths work with pure silver and use techniques such as smelting, forging, and engraving to create their artwork. Wood carvers use a variety of woods, including teak, mahogany, and tropical woods, which are prized for their strength and natural beauty.

These artisanal traditions are often passed down within families and communities, with the older generations passing on their knowledge and skills to the younger ones. Many of the artisans work in workshops or traditional village communities that specialize in specific craft skills and thus contribute to the preservation and promotion of Laos' cultural heritage.

By supporting local craft markets, cultural festivals and craft initiatives, it seeks to preserve and promote these traditional skills while promoting economic development and tourism in Laos. The artisan traditions of Laos are a significant heritage that not only reflects the artistic virtuosity of the artisans, but also conveys the diversity and depth of Laotian culture and history.

Folk Music and Storytelling in Laos

Folk music and storytelling have a long tradition in Laos and play an important role in the cultural life of the country. These forms of oral tradition are essential for the preservation and transmission of stories, legends and moral teachings that have shaped Laotian society.

Folk music in Laos encompasses a variety of genres and styles, often subject to regional and ethnic differences. A common form of folk music is the "lam", a traditional narrative song that is often accompanied by one or more singers who play on a khene, a kind of mouth organ made of bamboo. These songs tell stories about love, nature, religious themes and the daily life of the people of Laos.

Another important genre of Laotian folk music is the "morlam", which is performed at rural festivals and celebrations and is often combined with dance. Morlam music is known for its lively rhythms and melodic chants that create a happy and festive atmosphere. This musical tradition is often passed down from generation to generation and remains an important part of the social and cultural identity of many Laotian communities.

Storytelling is also an ancient tradition in Laos that serves to convey knowledge, wisdom and the moral values of society. Elderly people and storytellers play a crucial role in keeping the country's history alive by telling stories of historical events, legends of heroes and divine beings, and moral fables and myths.

These stories are often told at social gatherings, religious ceremonies, and cultural festivals to both entertain and teach. They serve to strengthen people's connection to their past and preserve Laos' cultural heritage for future generations. Storytellers often use rich language and vivid imagery to captivate their listeners and convey the moral teachings of the stories.

In modern times, folk music and storytelling are still living traditions in Laos, although they exist in a modern world shaped by technology and globalization. Nevertheless, they remain important means of strengthening identity and community spirit and celebrating the rich cultural diversity of Laos.

Education system and literacy in Laos

The education system and literacy in Laos have continued to evolve since the country's independence in 1954, although they continue to face challenges. The Laotian government has made education a priority area to promote the country's social development and economic modernization.

The education system in Laos is divided into three main levels: primary education, secondary education, and higher education. Primary education is compulsory for children aged 6 to 11 and includes six years of education. Although school enrolment has increased, there are still rural and remote areas where access to education is limited, especially for girls.

The literacy rate in Laos has improved, but is still below the average of other countries in Southeast Asia. According to UNESCO, the overall literacy rate is around 80%, with differences between urban and rural areas, as well as between genders. Literacy efforts focus on expanding access to basic education and promoting adult literacy programs to improve educational opportunities for all populations.

The Laotian education system also includes technical and vocational training institutions, as well as a growing number of colleges and universities that offer a variety of study programs. Most universities are located in the capital city of Vientiane, but they have limited capacity and need to evolve to meet the increasing demand for skilled professionals.

The challenges facing the education system in Laos include limited resources, inadequate infrastructure in rural areas, lack of qualified teachers, and the need for greater integration of modern educational technologies. The government is working closely with international organizations and donors to address these challenges and improve the quality and accessibility of education nationwide.

In conclusion, the education system and literacy in Laos are on a path of constant improvement, while the country continues to work to promote education as a fundamental right and engine for sustainable development. Progress in these areas plays a crucial role in the future prospects of the Laotian people and their ability to thrive in a globalised world.

Social Structures and Community Life in Laos

The social structures and community life in Laos reflect the diverse ethnic and cultural traditions that shape the country. Laos is known for its strong family ties and close community relationships, which play a significant role in people's daily lives.

Traditionally, Laotian communities have been closely linked and based on principles of reciprocity, support and cooperation. The family is the center of social life, and extended family structures are common. Older members of the community enjoy great respect and play an important role in decision-making and the preservation of cultural knowledge.

In many rural areas, people live in close-knit village communities, often centered on agricultural practices and traditional crafts. These communities maintain local traditions and customs, often celebrated through religious festivals, celebrations, and community activities.

The social structures in Laos also show a strong hierarchy and respect for authority. Older generations and village elders play a key role in conflict resolution and the mediation of social norms. Traditional Laotian society is often hierarchically organized, with respect for rank and age being of great importance.

With modernization and urbanization, the social structures in Laos have also changed. Cities like Vientiane and other larger centers have increasingly diverse populations and offer new social dynamics and job opportunities. This has led to a certain softening of traditional family structures, while at the same time creating new forms of social interaction and community development.

Laotian society is also characterized by ethnic diversity, with over 100 ethnic groups that have different languages, customs and ways of life. Despite this diversity, there is a common Laotian identity that is linked by the common history, language, and cultural practices.

Overall, social structures and community life in Laos are a complex web of traditional values, religious beliefs and social norms that shape the identity and coexistence of the people in the country. These structures are not static, but continue to evolve as Laos defines its role in the global community and preserves its social and cultural diversity.

Healthcare and medical care in Laos

Health care and medical care in Laos have developed continuously since the country's independence in 1954, but they face numerous challenges. Laos is among the poorer countries in Southeast Asia, which has an impact on health indicators and the availability of health services.

The health system in Laos is primarily publicly funded and coordinated by various ministries, including the Ministry of Health. Despite government efforts, there is still inadequate infrastructure, limited resources and a shortage of qualified medical staff, especially in rural areas. Many remote villages have limited access to medical facilities, which makes health care difficult for the population.

Health indicators in Laos are low compared to other countries in the region. Life expectancy at birth is about 68 years for men and 72 years for women. Infant mortality rates are also a concern, although they have fallen in recent decades. Infectious diseases such as malaria, dengue fever and tuberculosis are still widespread and pose a challenge to the health system.

In recent years, the government of Laos has invested more in the expansion and improvement of the health infrastructure. New hospitals and health centres have been built, especially in rural areas, to improve access to health services. Nevertheless, the quality of medical care remains a challenge, as many facilities struggle with limited resources and a lack of modern medical equipment.

In addition to primary health care efforts, the government is also working to strengthen public health programs and disease prevention. Vaccination campaigns, maternal and child health programmes and educational activities are central components of Laos' health strategy.

International organizations and non-governmental organizations also play an important role in supporting the Lao health system through technical assistance, training of health workers and providing funding for health projects.

Overall, health and medical care in Laos face major challenges, but there is also progress and commitment to improve the health and well-being of the population. The coming years will be crucial to further strengthen health infrastructure and make healthcare more accessible to all people in Laos.

Tourism in Laos: Development and Challenges

Tourism in Laos has developed steadily since the 1990s and is now an important economic sector for the country. Known as the "Land of Millions of Elephants," Laos attracts visitors with its unspoiled nature, rich cultural history, and spiritual sites. However, the country's tourism industry is comparatively small compared to its neighbors Thailand and Viet Nam.

The main attractions for tourists in Laos are the historic cities of Luang Prabang and Vientiane, as well as the country's natural beauties such as the Mekong River, the karstic limestone landscapes in Vang Vieng, and the waterfalls of Kuang Si. Luang Prabang, a UNESCO World Heritage City, is particularly popular for its well-preserved colonial architecture, Buddhist temples, and famous morning almsgiving ceremonies.

The development of the tourism sector in Laos has been supported by opening the country to foreign visitors and promoting ecotourism. There are a variety of tour operators that offer activities such as trekking, cycling, boat trips on the Mekong River, and visits to traditional villages to give visitors an authentic experience.

Despite the potential of the tourism sector, Laos faces some challenges. These include the limited tourist infrastructure, especially in remote areas, and the need to improve the services and quality of tourist facilities. The lack of diversification of tourism products and offers, as well as the seasonality of tourism, are also important considerations for the sustainable development of the sector.

Another topic is environmental and cultural preservation issues in connection with increasing tourism. Pressures on natural resources such as water and forest areas, as well as impacts on cultural sites, require careful planning and management strategies to preserve the uniqueness and beauty of Laos in the long term.

The Lao government is actively working to promote sustainable tourism and establish protected areas to preserve the environment while supporting the tourism sector. International support and partnerships play an important role in developing infrastructure and training workers in the tourism sector.

Overall, tourism in Laos offers considerable economic opportunities and contributes to the promotion of cultural understanding and international cooperation. The future of the tourism sector will depend on the balance between growth and sustainability to preserve the unique attractions and quality of life of the people of Laos.

Travel tips for Laos: Get to know the culture and enjoy nature

For travelers who want to visit Laos, the country offers a fascinating mix of rich culture and breathtaking nature. Let's start with the practicalities: To enter the country, most visitors need a visa, which can be applied for either in advance or upon arrival at the international airports. The official currency is the Laotian kip, although the US dollar is widely accepted in tourist areas. It is recommended to carry cash in smaller denominations, as larger banknotes are sometimes difficult to change.

The best time to visit Laos is during the cooler and drier months from November to February, when the weather is pleasantly mild. Temperatures rise significantly during the summer months from March to May, and the rainy season from June to October brings frequent and heavy rain showers that can make travel difficult.

For cultural exploration, Luang Prabang is an indispensable destination. This historic city on the banks of the Mekong River is known for its well-preserved Buddhist temples, including Wat Xieng Thong and Wat Mai. Visitors can experience the morning Tak Bat, the traditional almsgiving, or climb Mount Phousi for spectacular views over the city.

Another cultural highlight is the capital Vientiane, where the impressive That Luang Stupa and the Buddhist temple Wat Sisaket are among the most important sights. Here, visitors can also admire French colonial architecture and explore the lively market on the Mekong River.

For nature lovers, Laos offers a variety of options, from the picturesque beauty of the Kuang Si Waterfalls to the idyllic river landscapes of the Nam Ou and Nam Khan. The more adventurous can go trekking to the mountainous regions of the north or take a boat trip on the Mekong River to experience rural life and traditional villages.

The local cuisine is another highlight of any trip to Laos. Try traditional dishes such as the laap, a spicy minced meat salad, or the fiery Tam Mak Houng, a papaya salad. Rice is the staple food, accompanied by fresh herbs, vegetables, and meat. Fresh fruits such as mango, pineapple, and dragon fruit are also delicious snacks that are easy to find in the local markets.

When traveling through Laos, it is important to respect local customs and customs. Especially when visiting religious sites, appropriate clothing and behavior should be observed. Remember that Laos is a country with a rich spiritual tradition, and the locals value respect and courtesy.

In conclusion, Laos is a country that fascinates travelers with its variety of cultural treasures and natural wonders. With the right planning and openness to new experiences, visitors can experience an unforgettable journey here that immerses them deep into the soul of this beautiful country.

The main attractions of Vientiane

Vientiane, the tranquil capital of Laos, offers a variety of attractions that reflect the country's cultural heritage and history. One of the most outstanding attractions is the imposing That Luang Stupa, a national symbol and the country's most important religious monument. The stupa impresses with its golden dome that towers majestically over the city and is a central place for Buddhist pilgrims and visitors alike.

Another highlight is Wat Sisaket, the oldest temple in Vientiane, which impresses with its thousands of Buddha statues made of wood, stone, and bronze. The temple is an outstanding example of Laotian temple architecture and offers a glimpse into the country's religious practice and history.

In addition to these historical sites, Vientiane also offers an interesting mix of colonial architecture, which is particularly evident in the city center around Patuxai, the "Laotian Triumphal Gate". This monument was erected in honor of the Laotian fighters and offers visitors a magnificent view over the city from the observation deck.

For lovers of art and culture, the COPE Visitor Centre is a significant destination dedicated to supporting people affected by unexploded bombs and mines during the Indochina War. It offers insights into the history and humanitarian efforts to rescue and rehabilitate the victims.

Vientiane also offers charming ways to experience the local way of life, such as a visit to the lively Morning Market, which offers fresh produce, crafts, and local specialties. The Mekong Promenade is another popular place to stroll at sunset and enjoy the relaxed pace of river life.

The city has increasingly opened up to foreign visitors in recent years and offers a growing number of restaurants, cafes and accommodation to suit different budgets. With its relaxed atmosphere and a wealth of cultural treasures, Vientiane is a place that harmoniously combines both history and modern lifestyle, attracting visitors from all over the world.

Temples and monasteries in Laos

Temples and monasteries play a central role in the religious and cultural life of Laos. The country is heavily influenced by Theravada Buddhism, and its numerous temples and monasteries are important spiritual centers for believers and visitors alike.

One of the most important temple complexes in Laos is Wat Xieng Thong in Luang Prabang. It is considered one of the finest examples of traditional Laotian temple architecture and impresses with its ornate wood carving, gilded reliefs and elegant roofs. The temple was built in the 16th century and served as the royal chapel of the Laotian kings.

Another outstanding temple is the Pha That Luang in Vientiane, which is considered the national symbol of Laos. This golden stupa is an important Buddhist sanctuary and stands for the Buddhist teachings as well as the spiritual unity of the country. Pha That Luang is also the central destination of the annual That Luang Festival, which attracts thousands of pilgrims.

In the city of Xieng Khouang, known for the Plain of Jars, is Wat Phia Wat, which is also known for its historical significance and deep spiritual atmosphere. This temple complex is closely linked to the history of the region and the cultures of the ethnic groups that lived there.

In addition to these well-known temples, there are countless smaller temples and monasteries throughout Laos, often maintained by the local community. Many of these places offer visitors a glimpse into the everyday religious life of the people and serve as important social centers for communal prayers, festivals, and spiritual events.

The architecture of Laotian temples is characterized by its traditional elements, including the multi-tiered roofs, ornate facades, and ornate carvings, which often depict mythological stories and Buddhist symbols. These temples are not only places of prayer, but also works of art that reflect the craftsmanship and spiritual devotion of Laotian culture.

Temples and monasteries in Laos are not only religious sites, but also important cultural heritage that keep the country's history, art and spirituality alive. They offer visitors the opportunity to experience and understand the deep connection of Laotian society with its religious tradition.

Historic Sites & Museums in Laos

Historical sites and museums in Laos offer fascinating insights into the country's rich history and cultural diversity. Among the most significant historical sites is the Plain of Jars in Xieng Khouang, where there are hundreds of mysterious stone vessels that bear witness to an ancient civilization whose purpose and origin remain mysterious to this day.

Another outstanding example is the UNESCO World Heritage City of Luang Prabang, which impresses with its well-preserved colonial-era architecture and a variety of Buddhist temples such as Wat Xieng Thong. This city was once the capital of the Lan Xang Kingdom and has retained its historical splendor.

In Vientiane, the Patuxai, the "Laotian Triumphal Gate", is a striking monument that commemorates the country's independence efforts and rewards visitors with breathtaking views. The Presidential Palace and the Ho Phra Keo, a former royal temple that now serves as a museum, are other significant historical sites in the capital.

The National Museum in Vientiane is an important place to learn about the history and culture of Laos. It houses an impressive collection of artifacts, including Buddha statues, artwork, traditional textiles, and historical objects that document the country's development from prehistoric times to the present day.

The Champasak Provincial Museum in the south of the country is known for its exhibitions on Khmer culture and its archaeological remains, especially the UNESCO World Heritage Site of Wat Phu, a former Khmer temple complex dating back to the 11th century that sits majestically at the foot of a mountain and offers a glimpse into the historical connection between Laos and the Khmer Empire.

These historical sites and museums in Laos are not only the sites of bygone eras, but also living reminders of the country's cultural and historical significance in Southeast Asia. They offer visitors the opportunity to experience and understand the rich history, architectural masterpieces, and cultural diversity of Laos in all its glory.

The Mekong: Lifeline and Tourist Attraction

In addition to being a vital waterway for Laos, the Mekong River is also a major tourist attraction that attracts visitors from all over the world. With a length of over 4,300 kilometers, the Mekong is one of the longest rivers in the world and crosses six countries: China, Myanmar, Laos, Thailand, Cambodia and Viet Nam. In Laos, the Mekong stretches over a distance of about 1,900 kilometers and forms the natural border with Thailand in the west.

For the people of Laos, the Mekong is not only a source of fishing and agriculture, but also a central part of daily life and cultural identity. People use the river for transportation, trade, and as a source of water for irrigation systems that are essential for agriculture. The seasonal floods of the Mekong River play a crucial role in soil fertility and support the diversity of ecological habitats along its banks.

From a tourist point of view, the Mekong offers a variety of attractions and activities. A popular way to explore the river is by boat ride, which takes visitors to remote villages, ancient temples, and unspoiled natural landscapes. In cities such as Luang Prabang and Vientiane, river cruises along the Mekong River offer a relaxing way to discover the cultural and natural beauty of Laos.

Particularly impressive are the Mekong Falls in the south of Laos, such as the Khone Falls and the Pha Pheng Falls. These spectacular waterfalls are an impressive natural spectacle and a popular destination for nature lovers and adventure seekers. They also mark the border between Laos and Cambodia, offering visitors the chance to experience the power and beauty of the Mekong River in all its glory.

From an ecological point of view, the Mekong is a hotspot of biodiversity, home to numerous rare animal and plant species. The river landscape supports a variety of habitats, including flood forests, wetlands, and river arms, which provide important refuges for migratory birds and endangered species.

The Mekong River is also closely linked to the history and culture of Laos. Historically, it served as a trade route for goods and ideas between the peoples of Southeast Asia. The riverbanks are lined with ancient sites, Buddhist temples and traditional villages that reflect the heritage of the region.

In recent years, tourism along the Mekong River has increased, bringing opportunities but also challenges, especially in terms of environmental protection and sustainable development. The government of Laos is increasingly committed to the protection of the Mekong River and its natural resources in order to preserve the beauty and importance of this river for future generations.

Overall, the Mekong remains an indispensable lifeline for Laos and an inexhaustible source of inspiration and fascination for travelers from all over the world who want to experience its unique combination of nature, culture, and history.

Adventure tourism in Laos: trekking and rafting

Adventure tourism in Laos offers travelers a variety of exciting opportunities to experience the country's natural beauty and wilderness. Trekking tours through the untouched mountain landscapes in the north of Laos are particularly popular. The region around Luang Namtha and Muang Sing is a paradise for hikers, who can hike through dense forests and along scenic mountain trails to remote villages and ethnic minorities. These tours not only offer breathtaking views of the surrounding countryside, but also allow visitors to learn about the traditional life of the local population and take part in authentic cultural experiences.

Another exciting option for the adventurous is rafting on the wild rivers of Laos, including the Nam Ou, the Nam Tha and the Nam Khan. These rivers offer a variety of difficulty levels, from gentle currents for beginners to challenging rapids for experienced adventurers. Rafting tours lead through spectacular gorges, past lush jungle landscapes and along traditional riverside villages. The seasonal rains ensure optimal water conditions and contribute to the diversity of flora and fauna along the riverbanks, making these experiences unforgettable adventures.

In addition to trekking and rafting, Laos also offers other adventurous activities such as climbing in the limestone cliffs of Vang Vieng, known for its impressive caves and karst landscapes. This region is a popular destination for climbers of all skill levels who are looking for a challenge, surrounded by breathtaking views and the natural beauty of the surrounding area.

For nature lovers and birdwatchers, the nature reserves in Laos, such as the Nam Ha Protected Area and the Dong Phou Vieng Wildlife Sanctuary, are ideal places to discover rare animal species and diverse birdlife. Guided tours offer the opportunity to explore the region's unique biodiversity and learn more about efforts to protect natural habitats and endangered species in Laos.

Adventure tourism in Laos is not only a way to push the boundaries of one's comfort zone, but also a way to appreciate the unspoiled beauty of nature and connect with the country's rich cultural diversity. The government and local tour operators are working together to promote sustainable tourism practices that preserve the environment while providing visitors with unforgettable adventure experiences.

Experience spirituality: meditation centers and retreats

Laos has a rich spiritual tradition, which is reflected in various meditation centers and retreats that are open to both locals and visitors. Buddhism, which is the predominant religion in Laos, strongly shapes the spiritual practices and daily lives of many people in the country. Meditation centres offer an opportunity for inner contemplation and deepening of spiritual practice, whether for short retreats or longer stays.

One of the most famous meditation centers in Laos is Wat Sok Pa Luang in Luang Prabang. Here, visitors can take part in meditation classes and be guided by experienced monks. The place exudes peace and tranquility, ideal for meditation and spiritual reflection. A similar atmosphere is offered by the Wat Tam Wua Forest Monastery near Tha Khaek, where participants can immerse themselves in the practices of forest meditation, accompanied by the natural beauty of the surrounding landscape.

In addition to Buddhist meditation centers, there are also retreats and yoga retreats that offer a combination of meditation, yoga, and spiritual guidance. These places, often located in quiet and secluded settings, allow participants to retreat from the hustle and bustle of everyday life and gain deeper spiritual insights.

For travelers interested in spiritual practices, Laos offers a variety of opportunities to experience local spirituality and delve deeper into the traditional teachings and rituals of Buddhism. The country's spiritual centers and retreats are not only places of meditation and contemplation, but also important cultural institutions that contribute to the preservation and transmission of spiritual traditions and values.

Laotian Architecture: Temples and Royal Residences

Laotian architecture is a fascinating expression of the country's cultural and religious history, characterized by a mix of Buddhist, Hindu and traditional Laotian influences. Of particular note are the magnificent temples that can be found all over the country and play a central role in the spiritual life of the people. These temples are often surrounded by a peaceful atmosphere that attracts visitors and worshippers alike.

An outstanding example of Laotian architecture is Wat Xieng Thong in Luang Prabang, a UNESCO World Heritage Site. This temple is a masterpiece of traditional Laotian architecture, characterized by its detailed wood carvings, gilded facades and ornate roof structures. Temples such as Wat Xieng Thong serve not only as places of prayer and meditation, but also as centers of cultural activities and spiritual gatherings.

Another significant example is Wat Pha That Luang in Vientiane, the national symbol of Laos. This golden stupa, with its impressive architecture and symbolic value, embodies Buddhist teachings and the historical significance of the country. The stupa is a place of worship and attracts numerous pilgrims and visitors every year.

In addition to temples, royal residences play an important role in Laotian architectural history. The royal palaces, such as the former royal palace in Luang Prabang, showcase traditional Laotian architecture with its characteristic wooden architecture, lush gardens, and ornate interiors. These palaces are not only historical sights, but also witnesses to the country's royal history and culture.

Laotian architecture testifies to a deep connection with nature and a harmonious integration of art, religion and daily life. The structures reflect the region's traditional building techniques and materials, including teak, bamboo and bricks, which are carefully crafted into ornate structures and ornaments. Each temple and royal residence tells a story of the spiritual devotion and cultural identity of the Laotian people, and they remain an integral part of the cultural heritage that is preserved and revered to this day.

Traditional festivals and celebrations in Laos

Traditional festivals and celebrations play a central role in Laos' cultural life and reflect the country's diverse ethnic and religious landscape. One of the most important festivals is the Lao New Year, or Pi Mai, which is celebrated in April and lasts for three days. It is a time of new beginnings and purification, with people pouring water over Buddha statues and over each other to spread happiness and blessings. During this festival, the streets are filled with people performing traditional dances and organizing colorful parades.

Another important festival is the Boun Bang Fai, or Rocket Festival, which takes place in May and marks the beginning of the rainy season. It's a time of fertility and growth, and people launch homemade rockets to appease the rain god and guarantee bountiful harvests. This festival is accompanied by traditional music and dance and brings communities together to celebrate together.

The That Luang Festival in Vientiane is another significant event that takes place every year in November. It celebrates the That Luang Stupa, a national symbol of Laos.

106

During the festival, thousands of pilgrims gather to walk around the stupa, pray and make offerings. The festivities also include traditional dances, music, and cultural performances that honor the spiritual significance of the place.

In addition to these large festivals, there are numerous local festivals that vary depending on the region and ethnic groups. Many villages and towns celebrate Thanksgiving, traditional boat races, and religious ceremonies that reflect Laos' cultural diversity and heritage. These festivals are not only occasions for celebration and community, but also important events that strengthen the cohesion and identity of Laotian society.

Discover Laos: Insights into the daily life of the people

The daily life of the people of Laos is characterized by a deep-rooted cultural tradition and a quiet rhythm that is strongly influenced by the agricultural season and religious celebrations. In most rural areas, agriculture remains a primary occupation, with rice dominating as a staple food. Traditional farming techniques are passed down from generation to generation and are closely linked to the annual cycle, from sowing to planting to harvesting.

Social life in Laotian communities is characterised by mutual support and strong family cohesion. Families play a central role in daily life, and multigenerational households are common. Older people are highly respected and their wisdom is valued, which is manifested in traditional practices and expressions of respect.

Cities such as Vientiane and Luang Prabang, on the other hand, show a more dynamic picture with growing urbanization and modern lifestyles. In addition to traditional markets and Buddhist temples, you will also find modern shops, restaurants and educational institutions. The standard of living in cities varies widely, with some neighbourhoods showing significant economic development, while others remain more rural.

Religion plays a fundamental role in the daily lives of the people of Laos, especially Theravada Buddhism, which shapes the majority of the population. Buddhist temples (Wat) are centers of spiritual and social life, where believers recite prayers, make offerings, and ask monks for blessings. The spiritual life of the people is closely interwoven with their everyday practices, from the morning pasture collection to the annual festivals and ceremonies.

Traditional Laotian cuisine reflects the variety of local products and is known for its combination of fresh herbs, spices and rice dishes. Food is a social event where family members and friends come together to enjoy traditional dishes such as laap (minced meat salad), tam mak hoong (papaya salad), and sticky rice.

The education system in Laos faces challenges, but efforts are underway to improve access to education and increase literacy rates. Children often go to village schools, where they learn basic skills, while secondary schools and universities in larger cities offer higher education.

Overall, Laos offers a fascinating insight into the daily lives of its people, characterized by a rich cultural tradition, a strong family bond and the beauty of a largely untouched nature.

Future Prospects for Laos: Challenges and Opportunities

Laos faces a variety of challenges and opportunities when it comes to its future development. One of the key challenges is economic diversification and sustainable development. Although the country has rich natural resources such as hydropower potential and arable land, it remains one of the poorest countries in Southeast Asia with a high dependence on foreign investment and development aid.

The government of Laos has adopted several development strategies to boost economic growth and improve infrastructure. The promotion of tourism plays an important role in this, with the country looking to use its cultural heritage and natural beauty as a magnet for foreign visitors. At the same time, it is important to find a balance between protecting the environment and economic benefits, especially with regard to the expansion of hydropower plants on the Mekong.

Another key issue is social challenges, including access to education and healthcare, especially in rural areas. Despite progress, there are still large differences between urban and rural areas, as well as between different ethnic groups. The literacy rate has increased, but access to quality education and health services remains unevenly distributed.

Politically, Laos remains a one-party state under the leadership of the Lao People's Revolutionary Party, which raises questions about political freedom and freedom of expression. Efforts to achieve political reforms and greater involvement of civil society are in conflict with maintaining political stability and control.

In the field of the environment, Laos faces significant challenges, including preserving biodiversity and managing the effects of climate change. The protection of forests and other ecosystems is crucial to ensure the long-term sustainability of natural resources, which are central to agriculture and the ecosystem of the Mekong River.

Overall, Laos offers significant opportunities for economic growth and social development, provided that the government effectively implements its development strategies while addressing environmental, health and education challenges. Working with international partners and promoting sustainable economic growth will be crucial to shaping a positive future for Laos and its people.

Closing remarks

It is now time to bring this comprehensive overview of Laos to a conclusion. As we traveled through the pages of this book, we learned about the rich history, diverse culture, and stunning nature of this fascinating country. Laos, nestled between Thailand, Viet Nam, Cambodia, Myanmar and China, is more than just a geographical place; it is a melting pot of traditions, spirituality and hospitality.

The history of Laos dates back to ancient times, marked by legendary kingdoms that shaped the country and influenced its development. From the early Khmer regimes to the glorious era of Lan Xang to the colonial era and finally independence, Laos has taken a unique path through history. The decades of conflict and challenges of the 20th century, including the period as a neutral state during the Cold War, have shaped modern Laos.

Laotian culture is a living mosaic of traditions expressed in art, music, dance and crafts. The deep roots of Theravada Buddhism shape not only the spiritual landscape, but also the daily lives of the people. Traditional festivals and rituals reflect the connection of Laotians to their history and environment, while modern developments such as growing tourism and urbanization are bringing new dynamics to the country's social and cultural structures.

The natural beauty of Laos is as impressive as it is diverse. From the lush rainforests in the north to the fertile plains of the Mekong Delta in the south, the country offers a rich biodiversity that needs to be protected. National parks and nature reserves play a crucial role in preserving these precious ecosystems, which are not only vital to the local population, but also make a significant contribution to global environmental health.

The challenges facing Laos are as diverse as the opportunities. Economic development and poverty reduction remain key concerns, while the government is striving to improve infrastructure and attract foreign investment. At the same time, environmental concerns must be reconciled with economic growth in order to protect natural resources in the long term.

There has been progress in education and healthcare, but there are also challenges, especially in remote regions. Literacy rates are increasing, but access to quality education and health services remains unevenly distributed. Social structures and community life play a significant role in the daily life of Laotians, with traditional values and modern developments interwoven.

The future prospects for Laos are characterized by challenges, but also by opportunities. International cooperation and sustainable development strategies will be crucial to support the country on its path to a stable and prosperous future. The people of Laos, known for their kindness and smiles, face many tasks, but also full of hope and commitment for a better tomorrow.

In this closing remarks, I would like to thank you for taking you on this journey through Laos. May this book not only impart knowledge, but also arouse your curiosity and deepen your understanding of this unique country. Laos is more than just a destination; it is a treasure trove of history, culture and nature to be discovered. May you be inspired to explore the wonders of Laos for yourself and experience the beauty of this country.

Made in the USA
Columbia, SC
04 April 2025

56175616R00063